Carnival
An Imprint of HarperCollinsPublishers
77-85 Fulham Palace Road, London W6 8JB

Published by Carnival 1991

ISBN 0 00 192630 6

Art Direction and Design: Cindy Vance
Moral Support: Lisa Groening
Creative Team: Bill Morrison, Ray Johnson, Peter Alexander, and Steve Vance
Editor: Wendy Wolf
Legal Guardian: Susan Grode

FIRST EDITION

Library of Congress Cataloging-in-Publication Data
Groening, Maggie.
    Maggie Simpson's book of animals/by Maggie Groening and Matt Groening.
        p.   cm.
    Summary: Illustrations of the Simpson family at the zoo introduce such animals as the baboon, slug, lion, and swan.

    1. Zoo animals—Juvenile literature. [1. Zoo animals.]
I. Groening, Matt II. Title.
QL77.5.G674 1991
591—dc20

91-2866
CIP
AC

MAGGIE SIMPSON'S
BOOK OF ANIMALS

Maggie Groening and Matt Groening

Carnival

An Imprint of HarperCollins*Publishers*

MOUSE

CAT

DOG

HAMSTER

PEACOCK

BABOONS

MONKEYS

EEL

FROG

DUCKS

OWL

SKUNK

Maggie Groening, the original inspiration for the enigmatic youngest Simpson, writes books for children. She lives in Brooklyn, New York.

Matt Groening, brother of Maggie Groening, is the creator of *The Simpsons*™ and *Life in Hell* ®. He lives in Los Angeles.

Look out for all these titles published by
those good people at HarperCollins.

The Simpsons Rainy Day Fun Book.
Maggie Simpson's Concept Books.
The Simpsons Uncensored Family Album.